Casting Out
NABAL *and* JEZEBEL

Toward a Wesleyan
Complementarian Theology

Vic Reasoner

Fundamental
fWP
WESLEYAN
PUBLISHERS

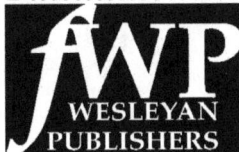

2120 Culverson Ave
Evansville, IN 47714-4811

ISBN 979-8-9916819-3-3
Library of Congress Control Number:
2026930028

TABLE of CONTENTS

Introduction 4
Equal worth – different roles 7
The American feminist movement 10
What about Wesley? 13
Feminism in the holiness movement 18
Recent Wesleyan feminism 21
Silent in church? 29
Christ and the church 32
Headship in the church 38
The Nabal spirit 45
The Jezebel spirit 47
Casting out both spirits 50
Revival in the home 58
Revival in the church 63
Bibliography 65

THE SPIRIT of NABAL
and JEZEBEL
Introduction

In the beginning God created marriage and it was beautiful. But it has been under attack ever since the fall. Two of the consequences of the fall, stated in Genesis 3:16, is that women want to control their husband and the husband will have a tendency to be domineering.

As a result of sin, a curse was pronounced against both male and female. In Genesis 3:16 God declared that Eve and the women who follow her will experience pain in childbearing. The Hebrew word עצב (*etseb*) describes intensification of labor and distress in pregnancy. Then God said the desire of the wife will be against her husband and he will attempt to dominate her.

This word for desire, תשוקה (*teshuqah*), is used in the Old Testament only two other places: Genesis 4 and Song of Solomon 7:10. Based on the use of the word in the nearer context, it would refer to a sinful desire to possess or control her husband. The phrase can be translated "your desire shall be *against* your husband." This is reflected in the English Standard Version.[1]

Even though the third reference is about sexual desire, it must be noted that Solomon's wife is describing his desire for

---

[1]See also Foh, "What is the Woman's Desire?"376-383.

her. Eve's punishment for her sin is not her sexual desire. It is a desire that did not exist before the fall. It is the desire to control.

But God's pronouncement to the male is also a curse. The ground is cursed and it is cultivated in pain. Here the Hebrew word for *pain* is עצבון (*itstsabon*). It describes labor and hardship in manual labor.

The ground will produce thorns and thistles. Man provides food for his family by the sweat of his brow. But in v 16 "he shall rule over you" is also part of the male curse. Adam was already the head of his family because he was created first (1 Tim 2:13). As head, he has the greater responsibility to protect and provide. But this verb *rule* (משל - *mashal*) in Genesis 3:16 goes beyond that responsibility. This verb means to have dominion — something they were to share — as stated in Genesis 1:26 and 28. In the first chapter of Genesis רדה (*radah*) is used. *Radah* is a verb about transferred authority. When men and women exercise *radah*, they act as God's regents. But "the sinful husband will try to be a tyrant over his wife."[2] *Mashal* is more tyrannical rule.

Dennis Kinlaw explained that Adam and Eve together chose a relationship of personal distrust, distance, suspicion, and disobedience. Because they turned their faces away from God, the result was a chasm, and God's face could no longer be seen. This amounted to a deliberate reorientation away from God and toward our own way. The result was a self-centered inversion; a kingdom within the self where the *I* could reign unchallenged.[3]

The effects of the fall on gender are evident in every area

---

[2]Hamilton, *Genesis 1-17*, 202.

[3]Kinlaw, *Let's Start with Jesus*, 111-125, 137.

of life. In Genesis 1-3 man and woman are of equal worth under God and co-laborers in performing the tasks of their Creator. They come together to have children. They rule over the earth as overseers of God's creation. Yet their failures are distinct because their created purposes are distinct. The woman abdicates her helping role by disregarding the Word of the Creator and disregarding the leadership of her husband. The man abdicates his role by disregarding the Word of the Creator and shifting blame to his helper.

Their punishment, therefore, was different. Gordon Wenham explained, "The sentences on the man and woman take the form of a disruption of their appointed roles."[4] The resulting issue for the woman becomes one of safety. It is difficult for the man to lead because the woman and the ground now "fight back." Therefore he copes by abdicating his leadership and focusing on whatever he perceives to be his competency.[5]

Before leaving the first family let us remember that Eve sinned first, then Adam. In desiring to be as God, Adam became less than man by submitting to his wife. However, the Scripture always holds Adam responsible (for example, see 1 Cor 15:22). Theologians often call Adam the "federal head" of the race. Adam was legally or federally the representative of the race.

What Adam was to the entire human family, each husband is for his own immediate family. The Bible is consistent at this point. The wife is under her husband's authority (Num 5:29) and the husband has "veto power" over any vow made by his wife (Num 30:8).

---

[4]Wenham, *Genesis 1-15*, 81.

[5]Talley, "Gender and Sanctification," 6-16.

Equal worth – different roles

At issue is not male superiority or female inferiority. Both male and female are created in God's image and are given dominion (Gen 1:26-28). The simple fact is that God is neither male nor female anatomically because he does not have a physical body. While I certainly affirm the incarnation — that at a point in time Jesus Christ took on a human body — in the beginning both male and female were created in the image of God. Yet God in his unity reveals himself to us using male pronouns. These male pronouns have been the basis for crusades to eradicate perceived patriarchal chauvinism so that women can realize their perception of full personhood. But they are in God's image fully without needing to become male.

John Oswalt explained that Yahweh is not sexual, although Israel's neighbors all had gods who were sexual. In contrast, God is transcendent. "Sexuality is a part of the creation, but it is not a part of the Creator." Scripture uses male terms to describe him, first of all because neuter terms were not an option since God has personality. But he is not androgynous nor are female terms used to represent him. Thus, we are left with male language. And we dare not tamper with it.[6]

Donald Bloesch argued that the debate over sexist language is ultimately a debate concerning the nature of God.[7] He explained in 1982,

Patriarchy preserves the biblical principle of an above and a below, of a first and a second, of head-

---

[6]Oswalt, "Why We Don't Call God Mother," 8-11.

[7]Bloesch, *Battle for the Trinity*, xv-xvi. Bloesch argues that there is no necessary correlation between grammatical gender and actual gender [p. 33].

ship and servanthood. To deny or erase these distinctions between members of the Trinity or between God and man or between man and woman is to end up in a pantheistic monism in which creaturehood is swallowed up in deity.[8]

Again in 1997 Bloesch warned,

Father language for God is being drastically curtailed and new symbols for God are being offered: the infinite depth and ground of all being, the creative process, the Womb of Being, the Primal Matrix, the pool of unlimited power, the New Being, the power of being, the Eternal Now and so on. Try praying to one of these![9]

According to Samuel Powell, if we continue to use traditional language, we must remind the church that they are metaphors. His other suggestion, Parent, Child, and Spirit, as Trinitarian language, is too ambiguous.[10]

Man is the generic Hebrew term, *adam*, for *mankind*. Nothing about the term *helper* in Genesis 2:18 implies inferiority. The same word is used of God in Psalm 118:6. *Weaker*, in 1 Peter 3:7, does not mean inferior. Because women are physically *weaker*, we treat them with respect, not contempt.

According to 1 Peter 3:1, part of her role is to submit to her husband, and if she does not submit to her husband *her*

---

[8]Bloesch, *Is the Bible Sexist?* 66,78-79; see also *God the Almighty*, 25-27; *Jesus Christ*, 75-79.

[9]Bloesch, *Jesus Christ*, 245.

[10]Powell, *The Trinity*, 178.

prayers may be hindered. The pronoun *your* in v 7 is plural. Since they are joint-heirs, either party may hinder their vertical relationship with God by being out of line in their horizontal relationship with their spouse.

The controversy in marriage concerns roles. Evangelical feminists want to abolish gender roles in society, church, and home. Their key verse is Galatians 3:28, "There is neither Jew nor Greek, slave nor free, male nor female, for you are all one in Christ Jesus," but they impose their own assumptions on the text.

The feminist argument is that submission is a result of the curse. Since the cross delivers from the curse, in Christ submission is no longer required. Therefore, marriage should be an egalitarian relationship with no male headship nor submission by the wife.

But this interpretation goes far beyond what Paul wrote. Galatians 3:28 affirms the basic equality of male and female, but it does not abolish their roles. The verse does not negate racial, economic, or sexual differences. The phrase *neither male nor female* does not advocate transgender confusion. The verse never mentions the husband/wife relationship. It does not change the relationship of husband and wife any more than it changes the ethnicity of Jew or Greek.

> The apostle's use of the male-female language of Genesis 1 in Galatians 3 thus makes it clear that he is concerned in this passage with the equality of human persons taught in the first creation account. He is not overturning the functional ordered relationship between man and woman that in other passages he derives from the Genesis 2 record of creation, in which man is created first and woman is created as his "helper" and "complementary counterpart," and the

language is "man" and "woman," not "male" and "female." [11]

Furthermore, submission was God's plan before the fall and was not part of the punishment. The institution of marriage was established before the fall by God and has not been abolished. In contrast, the institution of slavery was not established by God. It is the result of sin and is reversed by salvation.

The American Feminist Movement

The Feminist Movement or the Women's Liberation Movement advocates equal social, political, and all other rights of women to those of men. The first wave of this movement focused on suffrage or the right of women to vote. It rose out of an evangelical Christian context.

Mary Wollstonecraft was regarded as the first feminist when she published her book *A Vindication of the Rights of Women* in 1792. In 1848 the seventy-year fight for women's right to vote began. The Nineteenth Amendment was ratified in 1920. Susan B. Anthony was the most famous name associated with this early wave. She was also involved in the temperance movement against alcohol and the abolition of slavery. She was also pro-life.

The second wave of feminism developed between 1960-1980. Betty Friedan had written *The Feminine Mystique* in 1963. The National Organization for Women pushed for the Equal Rights Amendment and the focus was on abortion rights. Some of the best-known second-wave feminists were lesbians. Gloria Steinem swore that she would never marry, but she found the love of her life and married him at age 66. Typically,

---

[11]Saucy and TenElshof, *Women and Men in Ministry*, 146.

the second wave feminists deplored provocative dress as exploitation.

Now we are in the third wave of feminism. Typically third wave feminists utilize provocative dress as empowerment. In 1993 the Re-Imaging Conference was held in Minneapolis which culminated with an obvious substitution for the Lord's Supper or Communion. In a ritual called "Milk and Honey," participants were asked to pray that oppression of women would cease and a new religion would emerge replacing the old patriarchal Christianity. The chant was repeated,

> Our Maker Sophia, we are women in your image . . . With the hot blood of our wombs we give form to new life. . . . Sophia, creator God, let your milk and honey flow . . . With nectar between our thighs we invite a lover, we birth a child; with our warm body fluids we remind the world of its pleasure and sensations.[12]

Writing from a conservative Roman Catholic perspective, Carrie Gress concluded, "Feminism actually is not a subset of Christianity. It's actually a rival to Christianity."[13]

Among the options within feminist theology, some reject the authority and usefulness of the Bible, while others are loyal to the Bible but insist it cannot be interpreted to support what they deem as oppression. The revisionist type of feminism holds that the patriarchal framework of the Jewish and Christian traditions is a historic fact, but not theologically normative. Some feminists glorify life-giving and nurturing, and the

---

[12]Kersten, "Looking for God in the Mirror," 9.

[13]Gress, *Something Wicked* (2026).

Christian tradition is scoured for feminine symbols of God and the church. Still, other feminists are liberation theologians.

Evangelical feminists advocate for gender equality and the elimination of hierarchical, gender-based role distinctions that are based solely on sex. Few issues have polarized the evangelical community as has the feminist issue. On January 13, 1989 a two-page ad from the Council on Biblical Manhood and Womanhood appeared in *Christianity Today*. This council adopted the "Danvers Statement" in Danvers, Massachusetts which affirmed that men should bear the primary responsibility for leadership in the home and the church. Nearly fifty evangelical leaders and scholars were listed as either council members or on the board of reference. They contend that men and women are spiritually equal in worth but have been created with distinct, complementary roles and functions in life, including the church, home, and society. This view restricts certain church leadership roles, particularly those of senior pastor and elder, to men, while affirming that women are called to serve in equally important but different ministries

On April 9, 1990 Christians for Biblical Equality had a two-page ad in *Christianity Today* which took the opposite position. It was endorsed by over a hundred and fifty evangelical leaders and scholars. This perspective holds that gender should not restrict spiritual giftedness or leadership roles and that redemption in Christ restores the pre-fall unity between the sexes, allowing both men and women equal opportunity to serve. Egalitarians believe gender roles should be based on individual talent and calling, not on traditional or hierarchical views of gender.

Wesleyans were well represented in the endorsements for Christians for Biblical Equality. However, I am not aware of one Wesleyan scholar that signed the Danvers Statement or has identified with the Council on Biblical Manhood and Womanhood.

What about Wesley?

When John Wesley used women in the Methodist societies it must be remembered that Methodism was a parachurch organization. Wesley felt it was possible to do things within the Methodist society that could not be done within an ecclesiastical organization.[14] Methodist societies were divided into classes and Wesley did allow both men and women to be class leaders. He made it clear, though, that the class leader was to be under the pastor.[15] To allow a woman to exhort a class for four or five minutes was not the same to Wesley as preaching. Women were not allowed to take a text. This restriction implied that early Methodism preached expositionally and thus an exhortation was not regarded as preaching.

Wesley allowed for men to be lay preachers and still prohibited them from administering the Lord's Supper because they were not ordained. Wesley did not allow women to preach or administer the sacraments and to ordain them was unthinkable.[16] To claim Wesley opened this door to women is to misunderstand the Methodist system. Wesley never ordained a woman.

In "A Letter to a Person lately joined with the people called Quakers" Wesley stated the differences between Quakerism and Christianity. He took exception to Robert Barclay's statement that it was no longer unlawful for a woman to preach. He answered the argument that in the last days

---

[14]Clouse, "Introduction," 14.

[15]Wesley, *Letter* to Zachariah Yewdall, 30 May 1787.

[16]Wesley, *BE Works*, 9:573.

daughters would prophesy by making a distinction between preaching and prophesying. Nearly a full page is devoted to rebutting the error among the Quakers that women may preach.[17]

Wesley wrote Sarah Crosby, "The Methodists do not allow of women preachers."[18] Eight years later he cautioned her, "keep as far from what is called preaching as you can."[19] Wesley also wrote to Grace Walton,

> If a few more persons come in when you are meeting, you may either enlarge four or five minutes on a question you had, or give a short exhortation perhaps for five or six minutes, and then sing and pray. This is going as far as I think any woman should do. For the words of the apostle are clear. I think as always that the meaning is this: "I suffer not a woman to teach in a congregation nor thereby to assert authority over the man" whom God has invested with this prerogative.[20]

In his notes on 1 Corinthians 14:34 he may have given too much latitude when he commented that women are to be silent "unless they are under an extra-ordinary impulse of the Spirit." But Wesley understood that preaching and prophesying were not the same and may have had that in mind when he wrote the comment. He continued

---

[17]Wesley, *BE Works*, 14:311-312.

[18]Wesley, *Letter* to Sarah Crosby, 14 Feb 1761.

[19]Wesley, *Letter* to Sarah Crosby, 18 March 1769.

[20]Wesley, *Letter* presumably to Grace Walton, 8 Sept 1761. See Wesley, *BE Works*, 27:275.

For in other cases it is not permitted them to speak —
By way of teaching in public assemblies; but to be in
subjection — To the man, whose proper office it is to
lead and instruct the congregation.[21]

However, in his notes on Romans 16:1 he wrote,

In the apostolic age, some grave and pious women
were appointed deaconesses in every Church. It was
their office not to teach publicly, but to visit the sick,
the women in particular, and to minister to them both
in their temporal and spiritual necessities.[22]

The ministry of the deaconess was not an ordained office.
However, Wesley encouraged women and men to visit the
sick. He argued, "Herein there is no difference: 'there is neither male nor female in Christ Jesus.'"[23] His use of Galatians
3:28 in this context implies that he did think there were gender
differences in other areas.

It should be clear that Wesley allowed women latitude in
the Methodist society meetings that were not permissible in
church. In 1765 a question arose in an annual conference.

But how can we encourage the women in the bands to
speak, since "It is a shame for women to speak in the
Church?"

Wesley responded,

---

[21]Wesley, *Notes*, 440.

[22]Wesley, *Notes*, 404.

[23]Wesley, "On Visiting the Sick," Sermon #98, 3.7.

I deny, (1), That "speaking" here means any other than speaking as a *public teacher*. This St. Paul "suffered not," because it implied "usurping authority over the man." 1 Tim 2:12. Whereas no "authority" either over man or woman is usurped, by the "speaking" now in question. I deny (2), that the church in that text, means any other than the great congregation.[24]

Wesley explained,

The difference between us and the Quakers in this respect is manifest. They flatly deny the rule itself, although it stands clear in the Bible. We allow the rule; only we believe it admits of some *few* exceptions.[25]

Paul Chilcote argued that Wesley eventually loosed his restrictions against women speaking.[26] However, Chilcote does not take into account that this *speaking* was not regarded by Wesley as *preaching* and that it was allowed in society meetings not the great congregation.

Methodism did not become its own denomination in Great Britain until 1795. Wesley died in 1791.

After his death, Methodism became a church and there was "clear embarrassment about the existence of women preachers which led to the denial of ordination for women in

---

[24]Wesley, *BE Works*, 10:313.

[25]Wesley, *Letter* to Sarah Crosby, 2 Dec 1777.

[26]Chilcote, *John Wesley and the Women Preachers of Early Methodism*, 141.

the main Methodist church until the mid-twentieth century."[27] Thus, I think Chilcote exaggerates "the full recognition of a female ministry within Methodism during Wesley's lifetime."[28] Chilcote also conceded that Wesley "never permitted women's preaching to become a general practice."[29] He also reported that in a little more than a decade after Wesley's death women were either formally forbidden to function as preachers or severely restricted.[30]

Joseph Benson (1749-1821) served twice as president of the Methodist Conference and editor of the *Methodist Magazine* from 1803-1821. It was probably in October 1775 that Benson expressed disapproval that "any female whatsoever" enter the pulpit. This amounted to "breaking a plain command of God." He warned that if this was winked at for a few years, "we shall female preachers in abundance, more I dare say than men."[31]

In the United States Maggie Van Cott was the first woman licensed to preach in the Methodist Church. She was given a local preacher's license in 1869. In 1870 over seventy women received local preacher's licenses. However, in May 1880 the judiciary committee of General Conference rules that church law did not permit the ordaining or licensing of women and rescinded all local preachers' licenses from 1869 on. Full

---

[27]Maddox, "Wesleyan Theology and the Christian Feminist Critique," 109.

[28]Chilcote, *John Wesley and the Women Preachers*, 238.

[29]Chilcote, *John Wesley and the Women Preachers*, 171.

[30]Chilcote, *John Wesley and the Women Preachers*, 222, 236.

[31]Chilcote, *John Wesley and the Women Preachers*, 158-159, 234; Appendix E, 305-308.

clergy rights were not granted to women in the Methodist Episcopal Church until 1956.

Feminism in the holiness movement

In contrast, twenty-five percent of the clergy of the early holiness movement were women.[32] Here I am making a distinction between classic Methodism and the American holiness movement. This distinction is confusing because the holiness movement claims to be the legitimate heir of Wesley. However, they departed from his teachings at several critical points (they would say that they *improved* on him). That analysis is beyond the scope of this book, except as it pertains to the role of women.[33]

Charles Finney's Oberlin College became the first coeducational college in the world. Antoinette Brown Blackwell was the first woman in America to be fully ordained to the Christian ministry. Luther Lee, a Wesleyan Methodist, preached the ordination sermon on September 15, 1853.[34] However, Lee refused to perform the act of ordination or a certification to that effect.[35]

Blackwell had been influenced by Charles Finney and had gone to his school at Oberlin for undergraduate and theological studies. In 1849 she had stated her position in the *Oberlin Review*. However, four years after her ordination she became a Unitarian.

---

[32] Dayton, *Discovering an Evangelical Heritage*, 97-98. Maddox, "Wesleyan Theology," 109.

[33] See Reasoner, *Holy Living*, 2:533-647.

[34] Dayton, *Discovering*, 83.

[35] Kaufman, *"Logical" Luther Lee*, 166.

Another feminist at Oberlin, Lucy Stone refused to take her husband's name in marriage.[36] The correspondence between Stone and Blackwell during 1846-1850 was reprinted by Oberlin College under the title *Soul Mates*.

Phoebe Palmer wrote *The Promise of the Father* in 1859. The book, which runs 400 pages, argued that since the Spirit was poured out upon women as well as men that women have a right to minister. By appealing to Joel 2:28 she confused Wesley's distinction between preaching and prophesying.

However, Palmer did not argue for ordination, pastoral charge, or legislative authority for women. She also affirmed male headship, but argued that women have the right to speak when prompted by the Spirit.

B. T. Roberts, who was converted under Palmer's ministry and founded the Free Methodist Church, asserted more than he could prove when he wrote in *Ordaining Women*

In the New Testament church, women, as well as men, filled the office of Apostle, Prophet, Deacon or Preacher, and Pastor. There is not the slightest evidence that the functions of any of these offices, when filled by a woman, were different from what they were when filled by a man. Women took a part in governing the Apostolic church.[37]

W. B. Godbey felt a license or ordination was unnecessary for men or women and declared

It is the God-given right, blood-bought privilege, and

---

[36]Dayton, *Discovering*, 89.

[37]Roberts, *Ordaining Women*, 159.

bounden duty of the women, as well as the men, to preach the gospel.[38]

In 1881 Thomas Doty wrote in *Lessons in Holiness*:

God calls women to public services as truly, as specifically, as he does men. To-day is a pentecostal day, and the true pentecostal women are prophesying women.[39]

The *Manual of the Church of the Nazarene* in 1898 declared, "We recognize the equal right of both men and women to all offices of the Church of the Nazarene, including the ministry." However, ministry is more properly a calling, not a "right."

Alma White, who founded the Pillar of Fire Church, was the first woman bishop ever in the United States. She was ordained by W. B. Godbey in 1918. Her church, along with the National Women's Party, was the only other organization to endorse the Equal Rights Amendment when it was first introduced in 1923.

In an article on "Women in Leadership," Roberta Hestenes, herself an ordained minister, makes the statement that "leaders like John Wesley, Charles Finney, and B. T. Roberts affirmed full freedom for women in ministry."[40] The irony of history is that although the holiness movement was shaped by Finney, Palmer, and to a lesser degree by Luther Lee and B. T. Roberts, it claimed to be restoring the teachings of

---

[38]Godbey, *Women Preacher*, 3.

[39]Doty, *Lessons in Holiness*, 213-214.

[40]Hestenes, "Women in Leadership," 4-I.

John Wesley. The truth is that it differed from Wesley on many key points, including feminism. It was the holiness movement, not Wesley, that actually opened the door to feminism.

Milton S. Terry, a progressive Methodist, writing in 1891 reflected the historic Methodist belief by affirming male headship on three grounds: the basis of creation, that Christ appointed no female apostles; and apostolic prohibition stated in such passages as 1 Timothy 2:12.[41] Terry is famous for the classic work *Biblical Hermeneutics* (1883). However, by 1890 he had deleted whole sections moving to a more liberal position. By the time of his "open appeal" he no longer affirmed biblical inerrancy, but as late as 1904 he reiterated his support for male headship.[42]

Recent Wesleyan Feminism

In 1966 Roy S. Nicholson wrote in *The Wesleyan Bible Commentary*

> Paul's words do not negate the Christian principle of women's equal spiritual privilege with man, but they do set forth the principle of woman's subordination to man in the public worship of the Church.[43]

While Nicholson served as a leader in the Wesleyan Church, even filling the office of president, in 1996 the Wesleyan Church rewrote their *Discipline*. They deleted the long-

---

[41]Terry, *An Open Appeal to the Brethren [and] Replies Reviewed.*

[42]Terry, "Personal Relations to the Question of Higher Criticism," 426-427.

[43]Nicholson, "I & II Timothy and Titus," 5:584.

standing requirement for membership which stated, "To respect all duly constituted authority in the home." They also interjected gender-neutral language throughout the document.

Contrary to Nicholson's comments, the Nazarene's *Beacon Bible Commentary* (1965), which is also supposed to reflect Wesleyan doctrine, comments on the same passage but states a different position.

> We cannot accept the idea that even at Corinth the stipulations we have cited were to be applied in every case. . . . It would ill become us, therefore, to seek to base on Paul's remarks to Timothy a teaching that women are to be excluded from places of leadership in the church. . . . [The command in 1 Timothy 2:12] must be regarded as a demand imposed upon the church at Ephesus for reasons unknown to us. No universal teaching which would bind the Church for all time can be properly based upon it.[44]

Which position represents the Wesleyan position? How do we determine when a stipulation should be applied and when we should do the opposite? How can a commentator pretend not to know why Paul laid down a rule when Paul gives his reasons in the two subsequent verses? How can apostolic rule be considered binding only for a particular culture when the reasons given are theological and not cultural? The extent of the prohibition must be established from the text itself, not from modern cultural presuppositions.

The *Beacon Dictionary of Theology* (1983) questions whether scripture teaches a "chain of command" or hierarchy

---

[44]Gould, "I and II Timothy Titus," 9:576-577.

of headship and submission.[45] The article on "ordination of women" relies on Galatians 3:28 to remove all barriers for women. Apparently the rules were for Paul's day only because we have evolved to a higher standard.[46]

Also included in the dictionary are articles by feminist Nancy Hardesty which affirm "woman as man's equal companion in all areas" and which report on "women's liberation" in glowing terms.[47] Hardesty did not reveal in these articles, however, that she also advocates the rights and recognition of homosexuals and that her stand helped precipitate a split in the Evangelical Women's Caucus International.[48]

Writing in the *Asbury Bible Commentary* (1992), William H. Vermillion questioned whether the prohibitions in 1 Timothy 2 and 1 Corinthians 11 and 14 were universal. "This interpretation is one of the reasons why Wesleyans ordain women."[49] But raising a question certainly does not establish proper interpretation. Yet no solid exegesis is provided.

The study notes for 1 Timothy 2:12 in *The Wesley Bible* (1990) explained, "These restrictions may have been based on the inappropriate behavior of some women recently converted

---

[45]Brunk, "Chain of Command," 98-99.

[46]Clapp, "Ordination of Women," 376-377.

[47]Hardesty, "Woman" and "Women's Liberation" 548-549. A review of *Beacon Dictionary of Theology* in *Christianity Today* wondered "how objective a look at women's ordination can be gotten from Christian feminist Nancy Hardesty" ("Choice Books," 28:17 23 Nov 1984, 58).

[48]Spring, "Gay Rights Resolution Divides Membership of Evangelical Women's Caucus," 40-43.

[49]Vermillion, "1-2 Timothy, Titus," 1116.

from paganism."[50] Actually, v 13 explains Paul's basis and it is creation order. But that is not factored into the disclaimer.

The *Reflecting God Study Bible* (2000), produced by the Christian Holiness Partnership, stated that some believe the prohibition of 1 Timothy 2:12 "is not universal and permanent but restricted to the church situation. Under different circumstances the restrictions would not apply. Others believe that the appeal to the creation account makes the restrictions universal and permanent."[51]

This study Bible was actually an adaptation of *The NIV Study Bible* edited by Kenneth L. Barker who was dispensational and not Wesleyan in theology. The task of the Christian Holiness Partnership editorial team was to edit and revise the existing notes to provide a distinctively Wesleyan emphasis. The page format could not be changed. Zondervan accepted most of what was submitted. Somehow the possibility of a complementarian interpretation made it in.

The third Wesleyan study Bible, *The Wesley Study Bible* (2009), has "Wesleyan Core Terms." One of those is "women's leadership." There it is stated that Paul did not place women in lower positions than men. His practice of inclusion was also recognized by John Wesley in the early Methodist movement.[52] The study notes for 1 Corinthians 14:34-35 state, "Some doubt whether these verses were actually written by Paul rather than added by later scribes; in any case, they do not fit well into Paul's argument."[53]

The *Global Wesleyan Dictionary of Theology* (2013)

---

[50]Harper, ed. *The Wesley Bible*, 1820.

[51]Barker, ed. *Reflecting God Study Bible*, 1837.

[52]Green and Willimon, eds. *The Wesley Study Bible*, 1385.

[53]Green and Willimon, eds. *The Wesley Study Bible*, 1405.

declares that the two Pauline passages, 1 Timothy 2 and 1 Corinthians 14, "cannot be legitimately understood as universal commands that women remain silent in church. Narrow focus on these texts has often left the church advocating female exclusion that God obviously does not endorse and Paul did not practice."[54] But no exegesis is given of the passages to demonstrate how this conclusion was drawn. In the same dictionary, Ray Dunning stated that there has been a resurgence of female ordination in holiness churches.[55]

The *Global Wesleyan Encyclopedia of Biblical Theology* (2020) declares that "clearly the restrictions on leadership and preaching in 1 Timothy do not follow the practices of Jesus, Paul, or the early church. Rather, they have been imposed in a particular context for a particular reason and time."[56]

In the *New Beacon Bible Commentary* on 1-2 Timothy and Titus, David Ackerman identifies six interpretative options for 1 Timothy 2:12. He very adequately states the complementarian view and does not refute it. He then lists the contextual view that Ephesian women could not teach men is because they were uneducated, but the prohibition would not stand for educated women. The temporary ethic view was that Paul gave temporary restrictions until the influence of Galatians 3:28 could be realized. Fourth, the feminist reconstruction view says the text lacks authority because it interferes with the actualization of human liberation. The emerging ministry view holds that the passage must be read in light of other passages that discuss the fuller involvement of women in ministry. Thus, the passage deals with local problems in

---

[54]Lacelle-Peterson, "Women's Role in the Church," 577.

[55]Dunning, "Ordination," 375.

[56]Majeski, "Women Leaders in the Early Church," 417.

Ephesus and not other churches. Finally, the pseudonymous authorship view concludes that since Paul did not write this, some unknown author is trying to reestablish the patriarchalism that Paul actually challenged.[57]

However, in this 2016 "commentary in the Wesleyan Tradition," Ackerman concluded in his comments on 1 Timothy 2:12, "Paul does *not* prohibit women from teaching or leading. Early Christian women taught and had authority over men. They were not, however, to usurp the rightful authority of existing leaders in the church."[58] It is difficult to see how he arrived at that conclusion from reading the text.

Ken Schenck in the *Wesley One Volume Commentary* warns that we should not base our theology of women on 1 Timothy 2:11-15 because the precise meaning of the passage is hotly debated. Rather than contribute anything to our understanding of the text, Schenck merely writes that these verses are difficult because of prior assumptions of the gospel. He contributes nothing to a theology of the gospel or of women. Instead he reports that many scholars suggest Paul was addressing a local issue. Without contributing anything to the debate, he says that these verses belong in the category of unclear verses.[59]

The Next Methodism, published in 2021, contains 35 chapters which establish the trajectory of Methodism. Part Four: Our Public Witness deals with racism, sexual identity, and political theology. The other chapter in this section deals exclusively with the ordination of women. However, the only

---

[57]Ackerman, *NBBC*, 123-124.

[58]Acherman, *NBBC*, 121.

[59]Schenck, "1 Timothy," 834-835.

biblical citation is from Galatians 3:26-28.[60] Yet this is a core value for the next Methodism.

I have surveyed a dozen recent attempts to articulate Wesleyan theology with regard to the interpretation of 1 Timothy 2:12, arguably the clearest statement about the restrictions on women and ministry. None of them are convincing exegetically. Nor do they reflect classic Methodism.

Paul states, "I do not permit a woman to teach or to usurp a man's authority." The interpretative question is whether women are not permitted to teach error or to domineer over a man. In this case both prohibitions are negative. The second possibility is that both teaching and exercising authority are positive, but for reasons stated in the context Paul does not permit either activity. Or are both verbs actually describing one action — teaching in a domineering way. Is Paul denying these actions or this action for specific reasons when he would otherwise view such acts as positive?

Andreas Köstenberger concludes that Paul is prohibiting two separate actions, which are otherwise positive, due to special considerations.[61] At this point, he is likely to be dismissed, or at least ignored, by Wesleyans because he is Calvinistic. Yet his hermeneutical principles are rigorous and consistent with the general Protestant interpretive principles that early Methodism embraced. Before we disagree with his conclusions, we must at least engage his analysis, as well as other scholars who submit to the final authority of Scripture.

In contrast, the modern "Wesleyan" pattern has been generally dismissive of 1 Timothy 2:12, or at least superficial. Their scholarship has contributed virtually nothing. We come

---

[60]Deichmann, "Ordination of Women," 156.

[61]Köstenberger, "A Complex Sentence Structure," 91.

away with no help in interpreting the text. All we know is the authors' own biases. This is an embarrassment!

John Wesley affirmed *sola Scriptura*, that Scripture itself is our final authority. If we do not formulate our theology from an inductive study of what God said, then apparently we are free to formulate our theology based on sociology.   There can be honest disagreements on what the text means, but it is not acceptable to simply dismiss the text itself or treat it superficially. Wesley himself counseled, "Try all things by the written Word, and let all bow down before it. You are in danger of enthusiasm every hour, if you depart ever so little from Scripture."[62] If this is a minimal requirement for valid Scriptural exegesis, what did Oden mean in the introduction to his treatment of 1 Timothy 2:12, "This is a passage I have always disliked, resisted, and until now avoided at all costs"? In his defense, he proceeds to describe how the text has left its mark on his consciousness, in spite of his reservations. It is in this context that he promises his vague "middle way."[63]

Of greater concern today, a generation after Oden's struggles, is that the "next Methodism" does not reflect Wesley's counsel at this point. Their refusal to take a clear stand on biblical authority and inerrancy has left the door open to those with the audacity to tamper with the text. In 2 Corinthians 4:2 Paul says that Christian ministers do not δολόω (*doloo*) adulterate, corrupt, or tamper with God's Word.

For example, Kenneth Collins followed the example of his mentor, Thomas Oden. Oden did not affirm biblical inerrancy but constructed a consensus theology from those in the early centuries who did. In a similar way Collins has constructed a

---

[62]Wesley, *BE Works*, 13:112-113. Wesley's usage of *enthusiasm* would mean *fanaticism* in today's language.

[63]Oden, *First and Second Timothy and Titus*, 92-93.

Methodist theology from Wesley who affirmed inerrancy. But both men left their options open. They can be conservative when they agree with tradition and dismiss tradition when they disagree with it. While they reject more liberal theological conclusions they have undercut a more biblical exegesis by accepting liberal premises.

Silent in church?

The prohibition is stated in 1 Corinthians 14:34, that women should keep silent in the church. In light of Paul's statement in 1 Corinthians 11:5 which instructs a woman who will pray or prophesy in public worship, the statement in 1 Corinthians 14:34-35 that women are not allowed to speak must not be taken in an absolute sense. Paul has just required church leaders to evaluate the prophetic utterances. Women may participate in the giving of prophecy, but not in passing judgment in the assessment of these prophecies. They are not to ask questions, to object, altercate, or attempt to refute, according to Clarke.[64]

D. A. Carson concludes that women may prophecy but that they may not participate in the "oral weighing" of such prophecies, which is specified in v 29.[65] Apparently, those in authority were expected to discern whether or not an utterance comported with biblical teaching and women were not allowed to make such judgment calls.

Prophecy was not the same as expositional preaching. Both men and women could share what they believed God had brought to their mind for the good of the church — much like

---

[64]Clarke, *Commentary*, 6:279.

[65]Carson, "Silent in the Churches," 151-153.

our testimonies.[66] Nor is preaching a source of new revelation. Since the special revelation of Scripture is complete, and the canon of Scripture is closed, the offices of apostle and prophet no longer exist. Jesus is the final prophet and the New Testament is the deposit of their final revelation. Today, preaching involves the exposition of Scripture. It is such preaching that is restricted to faithful men.

In 1749 a book was published which accused Methodism of fanaticism. Wesley replied in the form of two open letters. In the second letter Wesley quoted the author, *"Women and boys* are actually employed in this ministry of *public preaching."* Then he replied, "Please to tell me where? I know them not, nor ever heard of them before."[67] This reply was published in 1751 and here Wesley categorically denied ever hearing of a Methodist woman preacher. It was included in the 1772 edition of his *Works*, edited by Wesley himself, without any caveat. What did actually constitute such preaching happened after his death in 1791 and before it was forbidden in 1803 at the Manchester Conference.

Since neither egalitarians nor complementarians see this "silent" as absolute, the one prohibition we must focus on is 1 Timothy 2:9-15. Kenneth Collins rejects this passage as a universal prohibition because women, no less than men, are equally created in the image of likeness of God. However, such a claim deals with the ontological nature of men and women, not their functional roles.

Collins then argued that since women are equally created in the image of God that they should not be barred from proclaiming the glad tidings of salvation. We must not retreat

---

[66]Grudem, *The Gift of Prophecy.*

[67]Wesley, *BE Works*, 11:406.

from Galatians 3:28.[68] But this does not constitute an adequate exegesis of 1 Timothy 2:9-15.[69] Furthermore, the Galatians passage does not abolish gender roles. It affirms the basic equality of male and female in Christ. Since inerrantists affirm differentiation of roles, Collins ends up rejecting the inerrancy of Scripture.[70] This is particularly troubling since Collins has devoted his academic career to the exegesis of John Wesley's teachings. Yet he has never exegeted Wesley's view of inerrancy because he does not accept it.[71]

Craig Keener, who also teaches at Asbury Theological Seminary (ATS), holds an egalitarian position on women in ministry, believing women should be open to all leadership roles in the church, including preaching and teaching. His view is based on the argument that biblical passages restricting women are largely tied to their specific cultural context in the first century, rather than an eternal command.

Ben Witherington, also at ATS, supports full equality between men and women in the church, including the roles of women in ministry and leadership. He argues that interpretations restricting women's roles are often based on cultural assumptions rather than the biblical text itself, and that passages like 1 Timothy 2 are specific to certain issues like false teaching, not a general prohibition against women teaching or

---

[68]Collins, *The Evangelical Moment*, 153-156.

[69]A major analysis of 1Tim 2:9-15 running 334 pages had been out ten years when Collins wrote, but he does not interact with Köstenberger, Schreiner, and Baldwin, *Women in the Church*. This book has contributions by eight evangelical scholars.

[70]Collins, *The Evangelical Moment*, 138, 142-143.

[71]McCarthy, "Why Wesleyans Should Embrace Biblical Inerrancy," 9-16.

leading. He believes the New Testament shows women in leadership and ministry roles, and that God calls women to public declaration of the gospel just as he calls men.

He argued that New Testament apostles, prophets, teachers, evangelists, elders, and deacons are not the same as Old Testaments priests. I agree, but Witherington fails to name any women who fill any of these six New Testament offices.[72] Nor do I object to women in ministry. The question is whether they are allowed to hold certain offices of leadership.

Christ and the church

The Bible never commands a husband to submit to his wife. Colossians 3:18, Titus 2:5, Ephesians 5:22, and 1 Peter 3:1 specify that it is the wife who is to submit. Ephesians 5:21 is often quoted in support of *mutual submission*. Even good authors often use this term carelessly. Both partners are to be considerate and thoughtful, but no institution can function without a system of authority. Someone has to take responsibility. Both cannot come under each other. A committee of two with no chairperson will not work! Besides that, Paul would undercut his instructions in the rest of the chapter if he meant "mutual submission."

Sarah Sumner sees marriage as an illustration of the relationship between Christ and the church, without mandating a strict hierarchical structure where the husband leads and the wife must follow in all circumstances. While she advocates mutual submission, she concedes that Ephesians 5:22-33 only tells wives to be submission. "It's conspicuous that the husband is never explicitly commanded to be subject to his wife."

---

[72]Witherington, "Why Arguments Against Women in Ministry Aren't Biblical (2009).

And there is no "mutual submission" between Christ and the church.[73] She also conceded that "mutual submission" does not preclude the church from having leaders.[74] For that matter, there is no mutual submission between parents and children, or even slaves and masters. Lincoln wrote, "Modern interpreters might perceive the first admonition as undermining or deconstructing the others, but clearly the original writer did not find them incompatible."[75]

Ephesians 5:21 is an introduction to the concept that everyone must live under authority. Then three examples are given: wife/husband, slave/master, and child/parent.

If one of the primary purposes of marriage is to symbolize the union of Christ and the church, then an egalitarian marriage destroys the symbolism. C. S. Lewis is often quoted as saying, "Only a man in masculine uniform can represent God to the church, since the church is essentially feminine to God."[76]

J. I. Packer said,

> The creation pattern, as biblically set forth, is: man to lead, woman to support; man to initiate, woman to enable; man to take responsibility for the well-being of woman, woman to take responsibility for helping man.[77]

Paul taught that Christ is head of the church and that the

---

[73]Sumner, *Men and Women in the Church*, 159-160.

[74]Sumner, *Men and Women in the Church*, 156.

[75]Lincoln, *WBC*, 42:366.

[76]Lewis, *God in the Dock*, 234-239.

[77]Packer, "Let's Stop Making Women Presbyters," 13-21.

husband is head of the home. Paul taught that the head of woman is man in the same sense that God the Father is head over God the Son (1 Cor 11:3). However, this Scriptural concept has given rise to the doctrine of the eternal subordination of the Son which can imply too much. Thomas Oden explained, "Subordinationism is that false teaching that argues that the Son is eternally and by nature unequal to the Father. . . . Any subordination that fails to recognize Christ's return to equality with the Father has not been ecumenically received." Oden then argued that the temporal subordination of Christ to the Father was voluntary. It was not based on ontology, since both the Father and the Son have the same divine nature.[78]

The more immediate issue in my discussion is how this Trinitarian concept informs the concept of marriage. A technical position called Eternal Functional Subordinationism has been utilized by come complementarians and rejected as heretical by egalitarians. Both sides seem to conclude that their opponents misunderstand them. I do not see that it is necessary to wade into this discussion any deeper. There was a voluntary subordination of the Son to the Father that is not necessarily eternal. The greater concept is that the Trinity has ontological equality and economic subordination.

The term *ontological* here means the eternal being or existence of God, his inherent nature, and the term *immanent* here means internal to itself. But there is also an *economic* Trinity. Not only is there a division of labor, but there is a subordination administratively in which God sends God. The Father loves the Son and sent him to earth. The Son prayed to the Father and was enabled by the Holy Spirit. When the Son returned to the Father, he sent the Spirit; however, Scripture

---

[78]Oden, *The Word of Life*, 82.

never speaks of the Son commanding the Father or the Spirit sending the Father or Son. Wesley explains:

> But we can no more infer, that they are not of the same Divine nature, because God is said to be the head of Christ, than that man and woman are not of the same human nature, because the man is said to be the head of the woman.[79]

Egalitarians emphasize the ontological aspect of the Trinity, while complementarians attempt to emphasize the economic or functional aspect — hopefully without denying the ontological aspect.

The magisterial theologians have used the analogy of marriage as a starting point in order to understand the dynamics within the Trinity.[80] According to 1 Corinthians 11:3, the Father has authority over the Son in the Trinity, just as the husband has authority over the wife in marriage. Both the Father and the Son are equally God from an ontological, or state of being, perspective. Yet in the economic Trinity, the Son submits to the Father. In marriage both husband and wife are equally created in the image of God ontologically, but the wife submits to her husband administratively.[81] John Fletcher used this analogy.

> For we who believe the divinity of our Lord, as it is set forth in the Scriptures and in the Nicene Creed, grant that as Eve was subordinate to Adam, so the

---

[79]Wesley, *Notes*, 430.

[80]Ury, *Trinitarian Personhood*, 276.

[81]Schreiner, "Head Coverings, Prophecies and the Trinity," 127-130.

Son is subordinate to the Father: but, at the same time, we assert, that as Eve, notwithstanding her subordination, was truly of one nature with Adam, the Son of God, notwithstanding his subordination to the Father, is of one nature with him also.[82]

Chrysostom warned,

If both had the very same roles, there would be no peace. The house is not rightly governed when all have precisely the same roles. There must be a differentiation of roles under a single head.[83]

Marriage is not only an analogy of the relationship within the Godhead, but marriage is also an analogy of the relationship between Christ and his church, the community of faith. If one of the primary purposes of marriage is to symbolize the union of Christ and the church, then an egalitarian marriage destroys the symbolism. John Starke concluded,

Despite the baggage of gender debates, "complementarian" seems to be the only good option in order to affirm in the Godhead both an equality in essence and an order of authority and submission among the persons.[84]

Marriage is perhaps the best illustration of the Trinity, although marriage is a double unity while the Trinity is a triple

---

[82]Fletcher, *Works*, 3:559.

[83]Oden, *ACCSNT*, 8:200.

[84]Starke, "Augustine and His Interpreters,"156.

unity. If two persons become one without losing their individuality, then why cannot three persons be one without losing their personality?

But marriage not only illustrates the Trinity, the eternal conversation of the Trinity reveals the dynamic of a healthy marriage. "We come closest to understanding God's inner life by attending to the intra-Trinitarian communicative action in the economy, particularly the dialogical interaction between the Father and the Son that is on conspicuous display in the Fourth Gospel."[85]

However, unlike the bonds of love within the Trinity, Genesis 3:16 explains that tension and conflict in the marriage come from our sinful nature. Adam Clarke wrote, "The husband should not be a tyrant, and the wife should not be the governor."[86]

Orthodox Christianity understands that Christ is of the same essence as God the Father. However, Christ did not consider his equality with the Father something to cling to (Phil 2:6). In the salvation order the Father sent the Son and the Son sent the Spirit.

Two lessons should be drawn from the harmony within the Trinity. First, husband and wife are of equal value to God in the same way that Father and Son are both God. Second, just as the Son willingly submitted to the Father's will, so the wife is to voluntarily submit to her husband.

Headship in the church

The Bible carries the doctrine of headship a step beyond

---

[85]Vanhoozer, *Remythologizing Theology*, 261.

[86]Clarke, *Commentary*, 6:463.

the home. In the Old Testament only men were priests and in the New Testament only men are to be pastors and deacons. Both are to be "the husband of one wife" (1 Tim 3:2, 12). God's standard for church leaders is that first they be in control at home (1 Tim 3:4-5, 12).

It would be a confusing situation if the husband was over the wife at home, but she was over him at church. That is why Paul stated, "I do not permit a woman to teach or to have authority over a man" (1 Tim 2:12). The fact that the verb *permit* is in the present tense does not mean that the command is temporary.

Every kind of teaching is not prohibited, however. In Bible times a teacher exercised great authority. Students were required to submit to the teacher who was an elder or community leader. What would be prohibited is the authoritative teaching of men by women. Titus 2:4, however, gives the proper context for women to teach.

This does not mean that a woman cannot or should not have a ministry. Neither is there any inference that certain spiritual gifts are not available to women. However, certain church *offices* are not available to women. Leadership is transferred to faithful *men* (2 Tim 2:2). *Men* is a masculine noun.

Recognizing that churches are structured differently and that the same terms mean different things in different settings, Susan Foh concluded that a woman may do anything except exercise the authority of an elder.[87] In her Presbyterian setting, elders rule and deacons serve. Thus, she allows for a woman to be a deacon or an administrator. Women may have delegated authority, but not leadership authority. Although governmental structure differs, her principle is valid. Gleason Archer

---

[87]Foh, "A Male Leadership View," 94-102.

wrote

> There is absolutely no reason to believe that Paul's prohibition is only cultural, limited to the women of a particular place and time. If teaching that is as simple and clear as this can be reinterpreted according to the moods and fashions of our day, then Paul's other inspired teachings may also be reinterpreted.[88]

Weinrich concluded that historically women were "learned and holy, but not pastors."[89] Köstenberger, Schreiner, and Baldwin explored the social world that is a necessary historical background in order to understand the first-century world. They also analyzed the term αὐθεντέω (*authenteo*), which literally means self-will. The word means "to have or exercise authority." They concluded that Paul wrote that the right of women to teach and their right to exercise authority over men was forbidden. This prohibition was not based on some culturally conditioned situation. Paul's prohibition was based on the fact that Adam was created first and that Eve was deceived. Paul does not explicitly say that all women are more vulnerable to deception, more prone to error, or lack the ability to teach. Rather, both reasons he gives are based on the order of events. Those who attempt to submit to Scripture at this point are not merely trying to uphold cultural traditions. Their commitment is based primarily upon the final authority of Scripture. They also concede there are gray areas in how this prohibition is to be applied. "We may concur on what the text means and yet disagree in some respects on how to apply

---

[88] Archer, "Ordination Is Not for Women," 8.

[89] Weinrich, "Women in the History of the Church," 263-279.

it to the variety of circumstances that arise."[90]

Anyone who accepts Scriptural authority, but not these conclusions, must bear the exegetical burden of proof. There have been at least a dozen feminist articles in the *Wesleyan Theological Journal*. Some are historical. Here I am more interested in the articles devoted to biblical exegesis.

Fred Layman began his 1980 article by stating

> Paul's teaching regarding women provides the greatest problematic for . . . all of us who attempt to work from a base in the New Testament when we deal with such matters as the relations between the sexes and with marriage.

However, the problem lies with feminism not Scripture. Sarah Sumner argued that there are no problem verses in the Bible since all Scripture is inspired by God. The problem is that Layman does not agree with the apostle Paul. However, Paul was inspired and Layman was not. To affirm *sola Scriptura* is to acknowledge Scripture as our final authority, not reason, tradition, or experience.

Layman took the position that *head* means beginning, source, or ground. It is supposed to refer to the fact that Adam was created first, not that he was placed in charge. Yet Paul's basis for female submission is based on creation order, not the fall (1 Tim 2:13). And we must remember *kephale* never occurs in that chapter. Thus, male headship is derived from 1 Corinthians 11:3 and is a separate argument.

Layman said the Greek word κεφαλή (*kephale*) corre-

---

[90]Köstenberger, Schreiner, and Baldwin, *Women in the Church*, 210-211.

sponds to the Hebrew word *rosh*.[91] But *rosh* is often translated *chief* in the King James Version.

However, Wayne Grudem surveyed 2336 examples of *kephale* in Greek literature and concluded the primary meaning is "authority over" nor "source."[92] In the Greek speaking world, to be the head of a group of people always meant to have authority over those people. Paul argues that the *head* of Christ is God (1 Cor 11:3). While Christ voluntarily submitted to the will of the Father, the Son is "eternally begotten" and is not inferior in essence nor in time sequence.

Sarah Sumner confirms that Grudem's research is valid. However, she argues that *kephale* is used either literally or metaphorically in these contexts. Paul has given us a picture not a definition.[93]

In a 1996 article Sharon Clark Pearson repeated the argument that *kephale* means source. She never interacts with Grudem's groundbreaking research. She concludes, "Whatever Paul's statement does mean, it in no way functions in this text [1 Cor 11:3] to limit the participation or leadership of women in public worship."[94]

In 2001 Diane Leclerc argued the feminist position based on the Wesleyan hermeneutic of love.[95] Her argument is developed from the tradition of Phoebe Palmer. However, she never establishes a specific "Wesleyan hermeneutic." Actually, the

---

[91]Layman, "Male Headship in Paul's Thought," 46-67.

[92]Grudem, "Does Kephale ('Head') Mean 'Source' or 'Authority Over,'" 38-59.

[93]Sumner, *Men and Women in the Church*, 150-153.

[94]Pearson, "Women in Ministry," 152.

[95]Leclerc, "Wesleyan-Holiness Feminist Hermeneutics," 105.

hermeneutics of classic Methodism were standard Protestant hermeneutics.[96]

At issue is not only *sola Scriptura*, but the grammatico-historical method. Feminism argues, "The Bible needs to be liberated from its captivity to one-sided white, middle-class, male interpretation."[97] Letty Russell concluded that the biblical text can only be considered to function as God's word when it is nonsexist and she admits that this puts feminism at odds with the historical critical method of interpretation.[98]

Elisabeth Fiorenza declared that "feminist theology must first of all denounce all texts and traditions that perpetuate and legitimize oppressive patriarchal structures and ideologies."[99] Obviously, the final authority of Scripture has been transferred to the final authority of such feminism.

The irony at this point is that while Paul argued that the first woman was deceived, he did not categorically declare that all women were gullible. However, feminism tends to declare that all men are helplessly biased. And they appeal to social justice, as well as liberation theology, as the solution.

When it is objected that it is impossible to exclude the interpreter's bias in the practice of the traditional hermeneutical method, it needs to be remembered that none of these proposed feminist models even pretend to be objective. In contrast to the grammatico-historical method, they substitute their own as a means of interjecting their personal biases. In 1986 Clark Pinnock called this "hermeneutical

---

[96]Reasoner, *Fundamental Wesleyan Systematic Theology*, 1:158-162.

[97]Russell, "Introduction," 12.

[98]Russell, "Introduction," 16.

[99]Fiorenza, "The Will to Choose or to Reject," 132.

ventriliquoism."[100]

In 1987 Randy Maddox did issue a caution about drawing sweeping feminist conclusions from historical generaliza-tions.[101] However, in 2020 Kelly Vargo attempted to portray Wesley as a proleptic feminist. She argued for a preferential option for all women, even cisgender and transgender women.[102] She would have done well to have re-read Maddox where he said that Wesley was convinced that women preach-ers was contrary to the *normative* teaching of Scripture.[103] Of course, Wesley said nothing to endorse sexual deception and perversion. On the contrary, he preached against it.[104]

In 2015 Hank Spaulding attempted to connect Wesley's theology of atonement with Womanist theologies of atonement. Essentially, a Womanist theology of atonement shifts from the death of Jesus, which they see as a coerced surrogacy role for the sins of humanity, to the life of Jesus. But salvation comes through his substitutionary death not his influential life. How-ever, Spaudling recommends that the Church of the Nazarene amend Article VI in their Articles of Faith to confirm with this supposed "proleptic" Wesley, which is actually anachronis-tic.[105]

---

[100]Pinnock, "Biblical Authority," 57.

[101]Maddox, "Wesleyan Theology," 101.

[102]Vargo, "A Proleptic Feminist Wesley," 127.

[103]Maddox, "Wesleyan Theology," 101.

[104]Wesley, "In What Sense We Are to Leave the World," Sermon #81, ¶18.

[105]Spaulding, "Sanctifying Atonement," 162-186. For a corrective, see Noble, "Feminist, Womanist and Pacifist Exemplarism" in *Christian Theology* 1.3:963-977.

The *Wesleyan Theological Journal* has never published a complementarian article. In Wilmore, the few who have dared to express their convictions concerning what they believe Scripture teaches have paid a high price. As a Protestant who affirms the right to private judgment on secondary issues, I honor their courage.

However, this complementarian truth must be balanced, by the caveat that no husband has unlimited authority. He is not God. Sapphira was judged by God because she did not disobey her husband. Acts 5:29 teaches that no person can take the authority of God. Both male and female are off balance and they express their sinful nature in their rebellion against the authority and submission which God established. In an attempt to break the logjam created when men blame women and women blame men, let us look at two pro-types which indicate how both genders are naturally sinful.

The Nabal Spirit

Nabal's story is found in 1 Samuel 25. His name described his nature. He was a moral fool. He was harsh and surly, as well as a drunkard. He was arrogant, egotistical, and rude. However, he was a descendant of Caleb, who was a great man of faith.

Commentators frequently say that Nabal was the alter ego of Saul, the major character in this section of 1 Samuel. David's primary battle is with Saul, but now he has an additional conflict with Nabal. The generic Hebrew word נבל (*nabal*) refers to mental deficiency. Saul had gone mad as early as 1 Samuel 16:14 and in order to avoid his paranoid obsession with David, David feigns madness himself in 1 Samuel 21:13. The stability of the nation rested in Samuel and as 1 Samuel 25 opens the first information we are given is that Samuel died.

In the midst of that mad world, Nabal's wife Abigail, however, possessed noble character. She ran interference for him, protecting him from his own lack of judgment. Hospitality was mandatary in that culture, yet Nabal withheld it, much like Ebenezer Scrooge who was too miserly to celebrate Christmas.

Abigail was prudent. She was perceptive and discerning, perhaps even prophetic in her statement at v 28. On the other hand, Nabal was so self-absorbed that he seemed unaware of his social obligations. Like Pharaoh, he hardened his heart and ultimately God hardened his heart in a sentence of death. He probably died of a stroke. His name sounded like the word for *wineskin*, referenced in v 18. According to v 37 he sobered up after ten days, but the text literally says "the wine had gone out of Nabal." This may be a wordplay. "In short, the man is equated with his bladder."[106] He was defined by biological functions. This may be a discrete way of saying that Nabal was full of it. If this sounds too crude, I refer you to the more literal KJV translation of v 22.

David asked a rhetorical question in 2 Samuel 3:33, "Should Abner die as a fool dies?" The Hebrew word *nabal*, which is translated *fool*, was the proper name of Nabal. David had not forgotten that encounter.

While the Bible does not provide much else on this marriage, it is significant that Abigail is a role model because of her *dis*obedience. In vv 24, 28 she confesses her guilt. She had no personal guilt, but was implicated through her husband's headship — much like the whole human race was implicated in Adam's "original" sin. However, her submission to this fool of a husband did not require her to be passive.

Thus, a proper concept of male headship does not imply that a

---

[106]Levenson, "1 Samuel 25," 227.

wife has no recourse except resignation.

The Nabal spirit manifests itself in its materialism, which can mean "boy's toys." Nabal is crude and governed by his biological impulses. Typically, feminists who have experienced abuse point to the chauvinism of a Nabal, while some men have been neutered by a Jezebel. According to Genesis 3:16 both tendencies are expressions of sin. However, neither gender has a monopoly on sinful tendencies, nor has either gender been exempted from the curse of sin. Martin Luther described sin as *in se curvatos* (the heart turned in upon itself).[107] Both genders are naturally self-centered. But this Nabal spirit must be balanced in light of the opposite dysfunction — the spirit of Jezebel.

The Jezebel spirit

Jezebel is the archetype of the controlling wife in 1 Kings 16-21. She was the daughter of Ethbaal, a pagan priest-king. She married Ahab to effect a political alliance between two nations, Tyre and Israel, in direct contradiction to God's Word. This alliance symbolizes the intermixture of the church and the world. Just as Nimrod is the prototype male to openly rebel against God, Jezebel is the prototype woman to do so.

The first reference in Scripture to Jezebel in 1 Kings 16:33 says that she encouraged idolatry in Israel through the use of Asherah poles which were phallic symbols. Through her influence the entire nation forsook the covenant, destroyed the sacred altars, and killed the prophets — except for a remnant of seven thousand who resisted her.

The historic Jezebel usurped her husband's role of leadership. She was haughty and proud. She usurped her husband's

---

[107]*Luther's Works*, 10:241; 25:245, 291, 313, 345, 351, 513; 33:175.

role. Although God's law forbade the king from taking Naboth's vineyard, she announced that she would not be stopped (1 Kgs 21:7-8). Just as Eve first ate the forbidden fruit, then enticed her husband to follow her, so Jezebel stirred up her husband to serve Baal (1 Kgs 21:25). This verb סות (*suth*) means to entice, to persuade and by implication to seduce. Thus, she connived to control a weak husband. She taught a pouting king who could not have what he wanted, in reference to the garden of Naboth, to look to her. And she committed murder to satisfy him and make him dependent upon her.

After his death, for fourteen years she wielded a significant degree of control over her son, Jehoram, but she is not mentioned again until her death in 2 Kings 9:30-37.

Her final effort was to intimidate Jehu after he killed Jehoram. Even though she knew her son had been slain, she did not put on a veil of mourning but made herself up cosmetically. Hobbs wrote, "She wished to depart this life in style!"[108] Unlike the proverbial description of "all dressed up but no place to go," she was not only dressed to kill but was headed the wrong direction!

Francis Frangipane wrote that the spirit of Jezebel is the spirit of obsessive sensuality, unbridled witchcraft, and hatred for male authority.

The spiritual of sensuality controls the world of fashion and entertainment. The spirit of witchcraft preaches power, not surrender. Those who serve her are eunuchs who are emasculated.

Look for Jezebel to target women who are embittered against men, either through neglect or misuse of au-

---

[108]Hobbs, *WBC* 13:118.

thority. This spirit operates through women who, because of insecurity, jealousy, or vanity, desire to control and dominate others. Jezebel is there behind the woman who publicly humiliates her husband with her tongue, and then thereafter controls him by his fear of public embarrassment. While she uses every means to sexual perversity known in hell, immorality is not the issue; *control* is what she seeks, using the power of sexual passion for the purpose of possessing men.[109]

The final reference in Scripture to Jezebel is Revelation 2:20. She is a false prophetess, connected to Balaam and the Nicolaitans in Pergamam. Both were attempts to infiltrate the church through a mixture of sexual immorality and spiritual adultery. Wall wrote, "Jezebel's heresy is the ancient equivalent of the current 'gospel of prosperity' that equate the gospel with present, material blessings."[110]

Her *sickbed* is actually describing sexual disease which results from being in bed with her. While there is a tradition that *Jezebel* was actually the pastor's wife,[111] her *children* imply that this same infiltration occurs within other churches. Furthermore, there seem to be parallels between Jezebel and Babylon, the immoral spiritual mother symbolized in Revelation 17.

This symbolic reference in Revelation brings the spirit of Jezebel from the home to the church. If a man has no purpose, ambition, or calling, he may in fact need a wife who has some

---

[109]Frangipane, *The Three Battlegrounds*, 111-118.

[110]Wall, *NICB*, 18:78.

[111]Reasoner, *Revelation*, 1:215.

sense of direction. But when a man is called by God for leadership, the devil can emasculate him more easily through a Jezebel spirit in his wife than by any other method. The feminist movement can be a reaction against overbearing men and fathers who have abandoned their responsibility. It can also become an expression of the woman's sinful nature.

According to 1 Timothy 3:5, if a man will not take the lead in his own household he is not qualified to pastor the church. He is disqualified from doing that which God has called him and equipped him to do if he does not have the voluntary cooperation and support of his helper. By living in harmony with her, he sets an example for the church. But if she has a Jezebel spirit, he cannot please her without compromising his own integrity. The result is that she becomes the de facto leader of the church. This controlling spirit works through manipulation. Manipulation, in contrast to force, amounts to yielding control without recognizing at the time what we have voluntarily done.

He cannot fight her like he would fight a man. He must respect the fact that physically she is the weaker vessel (1 Pet 3:7). But if he capitulates to her, she loses her respect for him and *he* becomes the weaker partner. A man who will not stand up to the Jezebel spirit at home will probably not be strong enough to lead the church either. The tension is that he cannot bat .500. He must lead at home *and* the church. A full-time evangelist once told me that half of all the pastors' homes he stayed in were unhappy and had marital conflict.

The average wife, however, has probably not made a pact with the devil. She may not even be aware that she is his pawn.

CASTING OUT BOTH SPIRITS

But we may be talking past each other. What does *subordination* actually imply? Yes, we must unconditionally submit to the will of God. But Acts 5:29 declares that we must obey God rather than mankind. The covenant institutions which God ordained amount to delegated authority. We are required to obey them conditionally. We may be required to disobey them when they usurp God's ultimate authority. Thus, citizens are expected to obey human government, but have the right to civil disobedience. How does this conditional obedience work in the church and especially in the family?

Before we can determine what submission looks like in the church we really need to define words like *clergy, ordination,* and even *preaching.*

Ministerial credentials, whether licensure or ordination, implies an endorsement based upon accountability. According to 1 Thessalonians 5:12, we are to know our spiritual leaders. When Paul would send liaisons to specific congregations, he would send them with a letter of endorsement or an inspired letter which contained such an endorsement.

For decades I have served on credential committees and sometimes chaired them. We have examined women who felt that God had called them to ministry. If God had called them, did they need our credential? In some cases, they were in a counseling or chaplaincy ministry which required such an endorsement. My attitude was never to restrict the "ministry" to a good-old-boys' club. My attitude was that they should be empower to do everything God had called them to do within the parameters of 1 Timothy 2:12. As Susah Foh pointed out, different church polities have different authority structures. Ordination, as I see it, is not a blank check to do everything in the church.

First of all, every Christian is a minister. Even within the Methodist tradition there was broad ministry opportunities for laypeople. A more basic and controversial question is whether there should be a distinction between clergy and laity. The distinction should be placed upon offices and roles. John Banks protested,

> Of all the transformations that history has witnessed, none is more complete or startling than that of the New Testament presbyter, with the simple function of religious instruction, into the priest in the sacerdotal sense.[112]

Writing in *Matthew Henry's Commentary*, Zechariah Merrill wrote that the word *clergy* is never restricted in the New Testament to the ministers of religion.[113] Today the term *clergy* is the general name given to those who are set apart by ordination. Without necessarily contending for the term, it is clear from Ephesians 4:11 that there were men who were separated to the work of the Christian ministry. Martin Luther taught, "It is true that all Christians are priests, but not all Christians are pastors."[114]

---

[112]Banks, *Manual of Christian Doctrine*, 299.

[113]*Matthew Henry's Commentary*, 6:1033.

[114]Krey, *RCS*, 8:122.

On the basis of the priesthood of all believers, Martin Luther believed that any Christian may bestow baptism and preside at communion. Luther also asserted the special office of the clergy in order to maintain church order and discipline. He believed that while all Christians are priests, only a few are ministers through their ordination.[115]

The ordination of women can only be addressed after we determine to what are we ordaining them. We first have to work through baggage like sacerdotalism. And the fundamental question is not whether women can speak publically or be endorsed for particular ministries. The fundamental question is how can this be done in a way that is consistent with male headship and authority. I am primarily concerned about a spirit which cares more about tearing down gender roles than it is about serving the church. I am primarily concerned with a spirit which dismisses Scriptural admonitions.

Even more basic is family structure. I once asked a woman whether she believed that she should submit to her husband? She replied that she did believe she should submit to him so long as she agreed with him! At the time I felt that her commitment did not imply much risk. And in the history that marriage, her husband proved to be wrong 100% of the time!

However, in a different situation, I was in a prayer group and shared with a fellow pastor some struggles. He offered to provide counsel for me so long as I agreed to do whatever he said. I thought that was the most ridiculous demand that I had ever heard. I was unwilling to surrender my personal responsibility, part of the image of God, and become a robot operating at his command. I later came to understand that he was influenced by the charismatic shepherding movement, which some regarded as cultic.

---

[115]Bloesch, *Essentials of Evangelical Theology*, 2:112.

I also knew a woman who started preaching at her local church because they did not have a pastor. Her unsaved husband was apparently embarrassed and forbade her to go to church. After praying about it, she decided that she should submit to him. I always felt that she had it backwards. He had no authority to usurp Hebrews 10:25, but she had no authority to function as the pastor. However, no one asked my opinion.

The word *submit* or *subordinate* means to come under authority. It is exemplified in the words of Mary, "Behold, I am the servant of the Lord; let it be to me according to your word" (Luke 1:38). This voluntary submission is also implied in the words of Jesus, "Nevertheless, not my will, but yours, be done" (Luke 22:42). *Nevertheless* indicates that he still had a will but that he chose to bring it under the Father's will. Just as Jesus submitted to God's will, so his followers much do the same. Christians are not in rebellion against God's creation order.

However, Mildred Wynkoop declared that surrender is not a biblical word and ought never to be used in relation to salvation.[116] When I first read her statement, I thought she was way off track. Romans 6:13-19 commands us to *yield* five times. Paul uses the same word again in Romans 12:1. The Greek verb is παρίστημι (*paristemi* or *paristano*). It means to hand ourselves over. This yielding to the will of God does not result in the loss of human personality, but it does involve the surrender of our will. I think that was what Wykoop was attempting to say. We really do not lose ourselves, but we need deliverance from our self-centeredness.

However, this verb *paristemi* is never used in the relationship of the wife to the husband — only in our relationship with God. Thus, our spouse is not God!

---

[116]Wynkoop, *A Theology of Love*, 178.

The Greek verb *hupotasso*, which is used in the marital relationship, implies obedience but allows for respectful disagreement. Every major New Testament passage which describes the relationship of wife to husband tells her to submit, but never tells him to force that submission. In Ephesians 5:22 the middle voice of the participle *submitting* indicates a choice made by the subject.[117]

Originally, *submission* was a military term meaning to take orders. But the family is not the army. We may be drafted into the armed forced involuntarily, but we enter into marriage voluntarily. The use of the middle voice emphasizes the voluntary character of the submission. So the question is what does it mean within a family relationship? O'Brien explained, "Different cultures may assign different roles for men and women, husbands and wives. What is important here is that the nature of the husband's headship in God's new society is explained in relation to Christ's headship."[118]

However, there is a stronger verb. In Ephesians 6:1 children are to ὑπακούω (*hupakouo*) their parents. This means to comply without objection. Paul does not use in the relationship of wife to husband. However, Peter does in 1 Peter 3:5. Peter wrote in 2 Peter 3:15 that Paul wrote some things which were hard to understand, which are liable to get twisted. Now I am reversing Peter's statement to say that *he* has utilized a word that could be misinterpreted! However, *all* Scripture is inspired — whether it came through Peter or Paul.

The interpretative issue is that words have to be translated according to their context. The word *hupotasso*, which is not as strong as *hupokouo*, had a military background. However,

---

[117]Reasoner, *Ephesians*, 294-299.

[118]O'Brien, *Ephesians*, 414.

the family is not a boot camp and military connotations cannot be transferred to the home. Likewise, a wife is *not* a child and this usage of *hupokouo* cannot be inferred to mean that a wife should be treated as a child.

In his comments on this verse, Wayne Grudem explained that the biblical submission of a wife does not mean putting the husband in the place of Christ. It does not mean she must surrender independent thought. It does not mean a wife should give up efforts to influence and guide her husband. It does not mean that a wife should give in to every demand of her husband. Submission is not based on lesser intelligence or competence. It does not mean being fearful or timid. It is not inconsistent with equality in Christ. It is an inner quality of gentleness that affirms the leadership of the husband.[119]

Of course Nabal has no interest in what the Bible actually says. He is contented to declare that somewhere in the Good Book his wife is commanded to do whatever he says. That is the full extent of his biblical knowledge!

But Daniel Doriani explained that *submit* is a more mild word than *obey*. "A wife who submits to her husband's guidance may still decide *how* to follow his directive."And "a believer's submission to human authorities is always qualified, never blind."

A submissive wife accepts her husband's leadership in general. She listens. She expects him to lead and does not chafe under the burden of following. She understands that submission does not undermine her dignity but expresses it. This is her unique opportunity to model Jesus, who submitted to the Father in the plan of redemption, even though Jesus is coequal

---

[119]Grudem, "Wives Like Sarah," 194-196.

and coeternal with the Father.[120]

I have purposefully cited Grudem and Doraini who are both complementarian. An egalitarian interpretation from the more liberal side might simply declare that Peter was wrong. But this is not an opinion for those of us who submit to biblical authority. Some egalitarians even work from an assumption of liberation theology. However, submission does not necessarily imply oppression — though a distorted view of submission may lead to oppression and abuse.

But the division may not always be in our understanding. It may be a heart problem. In 1984 Virginia Mollenkott wrote, "I am beginning to wonder whether indeed Christianity is patriarchal to its very core. If so, count me out. Some of us may be forced to leave Christianity in order to participate in Jesus' discipleship of equals."[121] Pinnock responded, "Apparently her commitment to feminism transcends her commitment even to the Christian faith."[122] Her threat to bolt sounds like a declaration of rebellion which was expressed further through her lesbian lifestyle. Thus, her religion was feminism, not Christianity.

When Lauren Schneider is willing to abandon Trinitarian theology, even monotheism, and reconstruct her own god in order to preserve her feminism, she has positioned herself outside orthodox Christianity. For her paganism is more attractive.[123]

Thomas Oden encountered this radical paganism, which

---

[120]Doriani, *REC*, 112, 119.

[121]Mollenkott, "Letter to *Christian Century*," 252.

[122]Pinnock, "Biblical Authority and the Issues in Question," 51.

[123]Schneider, *Re-Imaging the Divine*, 169.

he described in *Requiem*, as "an accommodation to syncretism in world religions that disavow witness to Jesus Christ."[124] Yet Oden defended women in ordained ministry and offered his own interpretation of 1 Timothy 2:11-12. He said that, "some view Paul's teaching about women at Ephesus to be so contextually defined, locally determined, and culturally conditioned that his instructions apply only to that situation. Others view the instructions as applicable to all times and all places, as Paul seems to indicate in verse 8 by the phrase "in every way." Oden then goes on to argue for an ambiguous "middle way," while having made a stronger case for "all times and all places."[125] The irony is that Oden, the father of paleo-orthodoxy, was willing to break with his own agenda in order to be "relevant" in contemporary theology. He very inconsistently argues for sexual inclusiveness in Christian ministry and devotes an entire chapter in *Pastoral Theology* to "Women in the Pastoral Office." He admits that "many will perceive [women pastors] as lacking the kind of historical consensus to which we have previously appealed" but he argues for an evolution of doctrine.[126]

Yet Oden is correct in his observation that there are varieties of feminists. Not all have the same agenda. I think the radical pagan feminists should be shown the church door if they do not leave voluntarily. On the other hand I want to treat my Christian sisters, who feel called to do something, with the upmost respect — even if we respectfully disagree over how much latitude Scripture offers them. For me the bottom line, the

---

[124]Oden, *Requiem*, 97. What he encountered was the aftermath of the Re-Imaging Conference described on p. 11.

[125]Oden, *First and Second Timothy and Titus*, 93.

[126]Oden, *Pastoral Theology*, 36.

irreducible minimum, is the final authority of Scripture. While we may have honest disagreement over the interpretation of controversial passages, I find it hard to respect those who are dismissive of the text itself. And in this context, my most basic question is whether there is any room in the "next Methodism" for those who are trying to submit to the biblical text and arrive at different conclusions from the status quo liberalism that has prevailed until now. If not, the next Methodism will very shortly look much like the previous Methodism. I prefer a return to the classic, original version that acknowledged biblical authority.

Revival in the Home

Since the most basic and foundational covenant institution God created is the family, this battle will have to be fought and won in the home first. The institutional church is off course because it is too often led by ministers who are out of divine order at home.

Men have a natural tendency to be overbearing, arrogant, and egotistical. Women have a natural tendency to control and rebel against male headship. So where do we start?

Revival begins with conviction, repentance, and forgiveness. Only the Holy Spirit can reveal to us the depravity of our sinful hearts. Too many nominal Christians have just enough religion to inoculate themselves against conviction and too much pride to keep them from acknowledging that they have been wrong.

The new birth, through the baptism of the Holy Spirit, will give supernatural power to rise above the sin that cling to us (Heb 12:2). Such sin has become our pattern of life and often it is passed on through example from one generation to the next. We can be delivered from fear. We have a new identity in Christ. We have been adopted into God's family and we have his assurance that we are his child.

But the old tendencies remain, even though they no longer reign. Dennis Kinlaw explained that the self needs to be liberated from the "tyranny of self-interest."[127] God's grace can enable us to love him with our whole heart and to love our neighbor as ourselves.

The Holy Spirit develops Christian character and maturity within those who are consistently led by the Spirit. Those who walk closest are the most conscious of their imperfections. Yet they can be cleansed at least from all conscious sin. The fruit of the Spirit can be increased in quality and quantity. They can have a greater delight in God's law and a greater consistency in keeping it. They may enjoy a greater sense of God's favor and blessing. They can develop a greater sensitivity and compassion for their neighbor.

According to Romans 13:1, God has ordained all authority. The word *ordain* describes an arrangement ordered by God. The word *ordain* in Romans 13:1 is τάσσω (*tasso*). It describes an arrangement ordered by God. Everyone must submit to authority which is over them. The word *submit* as used in vv 1 and 5 adds a prefix to that word *ordain* and means that we are to come under the arrangement made by God. The word *submit* is ὑποτάσσω (*hupotasso*). The prefix ὑπο (*hupo*) means *under*. Thus, *submit* means to come under authority.

What does all this have to do with holy living? We are to be models of submission to biblical authority. The opposition of submission is rebellion. In Greek it is the same word for *ordain* with the prefix *anti*. The carnal mind will not, nor can it, submit to God (Rom 8:7). The mind controlled by the Spirit has victory over sin (Rom 6:13-14). We must submit to God's

---

[127]Kinlaw, *Preaching in the Spirit*, 105-106, 108-109.

Word. We must submit to God-ordained authority in the home and in the church.

The holy life is most transparent at home. It is significant that there have been so many warped ideas concerning human sexuality and marriage which have been connected with sanctification. This may be part of the lasting legacy of Augustine. However, Ephesians 5 addresses the sanctification of the man and the woman in a redemptive marriage context. Here Paul teaches what it means to be a man or a woman in Christ as God reverses the effects of the fall within the context of the marriage relationship. Man was created to be the leader and initiator in his world, but he is now vulnerable because the world he was called to lead is fallen, and he is fallen as well. His tendency, therefore, is to fight back in an attempt to prove his strength and the appearance of competency. Thus, his focus becomes concerned with himself and not with those he is to lead.

The woman was created to be the responder and completer of her man, but now she is vulnerable in the area of safety. The man to which she responds may fail her. Rather than respond with an unfailing trust in her God and be the helpmeet she was called to be, she has a tendency to protect herself and become focused on herself rather than upon her husband.

Yet their relationship is to reflect the relationship between Christ and the church, according to Ephesians 5:22. The husband is to lead and nourish as Christ loves the church. The wife is to submit as the church submits to Christ. The call is for husbands and wives to "push back" the effects of the fall and live as redeemed men and women. The process of sanctification for the man is to put to death the fallen natural tendency to put his need for competency ahead of his wife's need for security. The woman must put submission to her husband above her own desire for security. She must learn to trust a man who can fail and she must try to uphold his honor. Thus both experience the process of sanctification as they fulfill their roles within the marriage and the marriage itself becomes a redemptive institution in which we are transformed.[128]

In his *Letters on Entire Sanctification*, John Hunt wrote in Letter 18 on family religion where he dealt with the duty of the husband to love, the wife to submit, and the children to obey parental authority. "A mature Christian will never have religion made a secondary thing in his family.[129]

Peter tells us that God's will for us is holiness (1 Pet 1:15-16). New Christians are exhorted to lay aside the tendencies of the sinful nature (2:1) such as guile, hypocrisy, envy, and evil speaking. Then Peter connects this with submission to God-ordained authority. After a section which runs twenty verses on submission, there is a description of Christian holiness, which is our calling (3:8-9). An unsubmissive attitude is a major tendency of the sinful nature. If the Bible actually prohibits women from teaching or exercising authority over men, a mark of biblical holiness should be to submit to the final authority of Scripture.

The first call of Jesus is "Come unto me."And yet the call to "come *after* me" (Luke 14:27) is a far deeper call to commitment and surrender. The cross teaches the brokenness of self denial. The imperative to *hate* in v 26 (Deut 21:15; Matt 6:24, 10:37; Luke 9:23, 16:13) means to love less. Jesus teaches that we must love him more than our reputation, than any relationship, than any possession, than any goal. He must be the center of our life. The real sin is the unsurenderedness

---

[128]Talley, "Gender and Sanctification," 6-16.

[129]Hunt, *Letters on Entire Sanctification*, 123-130.

of the ego. This sin is the root of all other sins. Self-surrender is both a definite crisis and a never-ending process since we can only surrender that of which we are aware. And self-surrender is the ultimate crisis because it is the breakthrough to spiritual growth. This self dies in order to truly live.

While most people are contented to live and die in awakened state, one of the characteristics of those who are truly born again is a desire to be holy. We yield or surrender to the level of light received. There may be many crisis moments, but there is an initial crisis moment when we first are convicted for our transgressions and another initial crisis moment when we are born again. Everything God does to move us away from sin, selfishness, and hell and toward goodness, sanctity, and heaven is a product of grace.

Entire sanctification is a pure love which loves God and man with our whole heart to the exclusion of everything contrary to that pure love. There is also an initial crisis moment when we first see our inner depravity, although the process of deliverance from it may necessitate many subsequent revelations and cleansings. There can also be an initial crisis moment when this love first displaces all sin. However, the believer who loves perfectly can still find areas in which he can be more completely conformed to the image of Christ.

This verb *cast out* in 1 John 4:18 is in the present tense indicating an ongoing process. As we trust Christ each moment we are cleansed by his blood and filled with his Spirit. The holy life is a moment-by-moment condition which is maintained by a moment-by-moment obedient faith. Thus, entire sanctification is a complete surrender to God, a deeper cleansing of our heart, a maturity of our character, and a perfect love toward our neighbor. Entire sanctification is purity, maturity, and consistency. It is discipline, stability, and character. It is holy love. It is Christlikeness. It is a heart cleansed from all unrighteousness, a death to self-centeredness, a perfection of motive.

Revival in the church

But heart holiness is also submission to God-ordained authority. A holy church is one which is comprised of holy families. The American holiness movement has not been much help in producing holy families. "Holiness" churches today are filled with the spirit of Jezebel and the spirit of Nadab. May God somehow help us to attain what we profess to have received already!

Jesus himself warned the church against the spirit of Jezebel. While I would not omit the spirit of Nabal, only Jezebel held the pseudo-official office of prophetess. Prophecy buffs are obsessed with the Antichrist. John taught that the antichrist spirit was present in the early church (1 John 2:18 - twice; 2:22; 4:3; 2 John 7). He is never portrayed in Scripture as a future world political leader. Instead, antichrist is in the church. While he comes in both masculine and feminine forms, the bottom line is that he or she, is lawless — dismissing the commands of Scripture. This spirit must be cast out. Any attempt at renewal must avoid simply reiterating the same spirit of rebellion that has brought down previous organizations. Every true revival will produce godly men and women who fill their proper roles in the home and the church.

BIBLIOGRAPHY

Ackerman, David A. *1&2 Timothy, Titus: New Beacon Bible Commentary*. Beacon Hill, 2016.

Archer, Gleason. "Ordination Is Not for Women." *Moody Monthly* 87:6 (February 1987) 8.

Banks, John S. *A Manual of Christian Doctrine*. John J. Tigert, ed. Nashville: Publishing House of the Methodist Episcopal Church, South, 1897.

Barker, Kenneth, ed. *Reflecting God Study Bible*. Zondervan, 2000.

Bloesch, Donald G. *Essentials of Evangelical Theology*. 2 vols. New York: HarperCollins, 1978.

_____. *Battle for the Trinity: The Debate over Inclusive God Language*. Ann Arbor: Servant, 1985.

_____. *Is the Bible Sexist?* Westchester, IL: Crossway, 1982.

_____. *Christian Foundations: Jesus Christ: Savior and Lord*. Downers Grove, IL: InterVarsity, 1997.

_____. *Christian Foundations: God the Almighty*. Downers Grove, IL: InterVarsity, 1995.

Brunk, George R. III. "Chain of Command." *Beacon Dictionary of Theology*. Richard S. Taylor, ed. Beacon Hill, 1983.

Carson, D. A. "Silent in the Churches." *Recovering Biblical Manhood and Womanhood*. John Piper and Wayne Grudem, eds. Crossway, 1991.

Chilcote, Paul Wesley. *John Wesley and the Women Preachers of Early Methodism*. Scarecrow, 1991.

Clapp, Philip S. "Ordination of Women." *Beacon Dictionary of Theology*. Richard S. Taylor, ed. Beacon Hill, 1983.

Clouse, Robert G. "Introduction." *Women in Ministry: Four Views*. Bonnidell Clouse and Robert G. Clouse, eds. InterVarsity, 1989.

Collins, Kenneth J. *The Evangelical Moment: The Promise of an American Religion*. Baker, 2005.

Dayton, Donald W. *Discovering An Evangelical Heritage*. Harper and Row, 1976.

Deichmann, Wendy J. "Ordination of Women." *The NextMethodism*. Kenneth J. Collins and Ryan N. Danker, eds. Seedbed, 2021.

Doriani, Daniel M. *Reformed Expository Commentary: 1 Peter*. Phillipsburg, NJ: P&R, 2014 [*REC*].

Doty, Thomas K. *Lessons in Holiness*. 1881. Reprint, Schmul, 2024.

Dunning, H. Ray. "Ordination." *Global Wesleyan Dictionary of Theology*. Al Truesdale, ed. Beacon Hill, 2013.

Fiorenza, Elisabeth Schüssler. "The Will to Choose or to Reject: Continuing Our Critical Work." *Feminist Interpretation of the Bible*. Philadelphia: Westminster, 1985.

Fletcher, John. *The Works of the Reverend John Fletcher*. 1833. Reprint, Schmul, 1974.

Foh, Susan T. "A Male Leadership View." *Women in Ministry: Four Views*. Bonnidell Clouse and Robert G. Clouse, eds. InterVarsity, 1989.

_____. "What is the Woman's Desire?" *Westminster Theological Journal* 37 (1974/75) 376-383.

Frangipane, Francis. *The Three Battlegrounds*. Charolette:

Arrow, 1989.

Green Joel B. and William H. Willimon, eds. *The Wesley Study Bible.* Abingdon, 2009.

Gress, Carrie. *Something Wicked: Why Feminism Can't Be Fused With Christianity.* Manchester, NH: Sophia Institute Press, 2026.

Godbey, W. B. *Women Preacher.* Pentecostal, 1891.

Gould, J. Glen. "I and II Timothy, Titus." *Beacon Bible Commentary.* Vol. 9. Beacon Hill, 1965.

Grudem, Wayne. *The Gift of Prophecy: In the New Testament and Today.* Crossway, 1988.

_____. "Does Kephale ('Head') Mean 'Source' or 'Authority Over' in Greek Literature? A Survey of 2,336 Examples." *Trinity Journal,* 6 NS (1985) 38-59.

_____. "Wives Like Sarah, and Husbands Who Honor Them" in *Recovering Biblical Manhood & Womanhood.* John Piper and Wayne Grudem, eds. Wheaton, IL: Crossway, 1991.

Hamilton, Victor P. *The Book of Genesis Chapters 1-17: New International Commentary on the Old Testament.* Eerdmans, 1990.

Hardesty, Nancy A. "Woman" and "Women's Liberation." *Beacon Dictionary of Theology.* Richard S. Taylor, ed. Beacon Hill, 1983.

Harper, Albert F. ed. *The Wesley Bible.* Thomas Nelson, 1990.

Henry, Matthew. *Commentary on the Whole Bible.* 6 vols. 1708-1710. Reprint, McLean, VA: MacDonald, 198-.

Hestenes, Roberta. "Women in Leadership: Finding Ways to Serve the Church." *Christianity Today* 30:14 (3 October 1986) 4-I–10-I.

Hobbs, T. R. *2 Kings: Word Biblical Commentary.* Word, 1985.

Hunt, John. *Letters on Entire Sanctification*. 1849. Reprint, Schmul, 1984 as *Letters on Sanctification*.

Kaufman, Paul Leslie. *"Logical" Luther Lee and the Methodist War Against Slavery*. Scarecrow, 2000.

Keener, Craig S. *Paul, Women and Wives: Marriage and Women's Ministry in the Letters of Paul*. Hendrickson, 1992.

Kersten, Katherine. "Looking for God in the Mirror." *Faith & Freedom* (Spring 1994) 8-9.

Kinlaw, Dennis F. *Let's Start with Jesus*. Zondervan, 2005.

_____. *Preaching in the Spirit*. Francis Asbury Press, 1985.

Köstenberger, Andreas J, Thomas R. Schreiner, and H. Scott Baldwin. *Women in the Church: A Fresh Analysis of 1 Timothy 2:9-15*. Baker. 1995. Köstenberger. "A Complex Sentence Structure" in a chapter in this book.

Krey, Philip D. W. and Peter D. S. Krey, eds. *Reformation Commentary on Scripture: Romans 9-16*. Vol. 8. Downers Grove, IL: InterVarsity, 2016 [*RCS*].

Lacelle-Peterson, Kristina. "Women's Role in the Church." *Global Wesleyan Dictionary of Theology*. Al Truesdale, ed. Beacon Hill, 2013.

Layman, Fred D. "Male Headship in Paul's Thought." *Wesleyan Theological Journal* 15:1 (Spring, 1980) 46-67.

Leclerc, Diane "Wesleyan-Holiness Feminist Hermeneutics: Historical Rendering, Current Considerations." Wesleyan Theological Journal 36:2 (Fall 2001) 105-132.

Levenson, Jon D. "1 Samuel 25 as Literature and History." *Literary Interpretations of Biblical Narratives*. Kenneth R. R. Gros Louis, ed. Abingdon, 1982. 2:220-242.

Lewis, C. S. *God in the Dock*. 1970. Reprint, Eerdmans, 2014.

Lincoln, Andrew T. *Ephesians. Word Biblical Commen-*

tary. Vol. 42. Dallas, TX: Word, 1990 [*WBC*].

Luther, Martin. *Luther's Works*. American ed. 79 vols. Javoslav Pelikan and Helmut T. Lehmann, eds. St. Louis: Concordia, 1955-2016.

Maddox, Randy L. "Wesleyan Theology and the Christian Feminist Critique." *Wesleyan Theological Journal*, 22:1 (Spring 1987) 100-110.

Majeski, Kimberly S. "Women Leaders in the Early Church and 1 Timothy 2." *Global Wesleyan Encyclopedia of Biblical Theology*. Robert . D. Branson, ed. The Foundry, 2020.

McCarthy Daryl E. "Why Wesleyans Should Embrace Biblical Inerrancy: Reflections on Kenneth Collins' Article 'Should Wesleyans Embrace a Doctrine of Inerrancy?'" *The Arminian Magazine* 42:2 (Fall 2024) 9-15.

Mollenkott, Virginia. "Letter to *Christian Century*." (7 March 1984) 252.

Nicholson, Roy S. "I & II Timothy and Titus." *The Wesleyan Bible Commentary*. Vol. 5. Charles W. Carter, ed. Baker, 1966.

Noble, Thomas A. *Christian Theology*. Vol 1. *The Grace of our Lord Jesus Christ*. The Foundry, 2022.

Oden, Thomas C. ed. *Ancient Christian Commentary on Scripture*. 29 vols. InterVarsity, 1998-2010. [*ACCS*]

_____. *The Word of Life: Systematic Theology: Volume Two*. Harper & Row, 1989.

_____. *First and Second Timothy and Titus: Interpretation: A Bible Commentary for Teaching and Preaching*. Louisville: John Knox Press, 1989.

_____. *Requiem: A Lament in Three Movements*. Nashville: Abingdon, 1995.

_____. *Pastoral Theology*. San Francisco: Harper & Row, 1983.

Oswalt, John N. "Why We Don't Call God Mother." *High Calling* (Sept-Oct 2013) 8-11.

Packer, James I. "Let's Stop Making Women Presbyters." *Christianity Today* 35:2 (11 Feb 1991) 13-21.

Pearson, Sharon Clark. "Women in Ministry: A Biblical Vision." *Wesleyan Theological Journal* 31:1 (Spring 1996) 141-170.

Pinnock, Clark H. "Biblical Authority and the Issues in Question." *Women, Authority and the Bible*. Alvera Mickelsen, ed. Downers Grove, IL: InterVarsity, 1986.

Powell, Samuel M. *The Trinity: Wesleyan Theology Series*. Kansas City: The Foundry, 2020.

Reasoner, Vic. *A Fundamental Wesleyan Commentary on Revelation 1-9*. 2nd ed. Fundamental Wesleyan, 2023.

_____. *Fundamental Wesleyan Systematic Theology*. Fundamental Wesleyan, 2021.

_____. *A Fundamental Wesleyan Commentary on Ephesians*. Fundamental Wesleyan, 2020.

_____. *A Wesleyan Theology of Holy Living for the Twenty-first Century*. 2 vols. Evansville, IN: Fundamental Wesleyan 2012.

Roberts, B. T. *Ordaining Women*. Earnest Christian, 1891.

Russell, Letty M. "Introduction: Liberating the Word." *Feminist Interpretation of the Bible*. Philadelphia: Westminster, 1985.

Saucy, Robert L. and Judith TenElshof, eds. *Women and Men in Ministry: A Complementary Perspective*. Chicago: Moody, 2001.

Schenck, Ken. "1 Timothy." *Wesley One Volume Commentary*. Kenneth J. Collins and Robert W. Wall, eds. Nashville: Abingdon, 2020.

Schneider, Laurel C. *Re-Imaging the Divine: Confronting the Backlash Against Feminist Theology*. Cleveland:

Pilgrim Press, 1998.

Schreiner, Thomas R. "Head Coverings, Prophecies and the Trinity: 1 Corinthians 11:2-16." *Recovering Biblical Manhood and Womanhood*. John Piper and Wayne Grudem, eds. Crossway, 1991.

Spaulding, Hank. "Sanctifying Atonement: Womanist Theology, Wesleyan Ethics, and the Future of Nazarene Atonement Theology. *Wesleyan Theological Journal* 50:1 (Spring 2015) 162-186.

Spring, Beth. "Gay Rights Resolution Divides Membership of Evangelical Women's Caucus." *Christianity Today* 30:14 (3 October 1986) 40-43.

Starke, John. "Augustine and His Interpreters." *One God in Three Persons*. Bruce A. Ware and John Starke, eds. Crossway, 2015.

Sumner, Sarah. *Men and Women in the Church*. Downers Grove, IL: InterVarsity, 2003.

Talley, David Lee. "Gender and Sanctification: From Creation to Transformation." *Journal of Manhood and Womanhood* 8:1 (Spring 1987) 71-77.

Terry, Milton S. *An Open Appeal to the Brethren [and] Replies Reviewed*. 1891. 8 pages. Reprinted from *Christian Advocate* 66:11 (12 March 1891) 170 and *Christian Advocate* 66:35 (27 Aug 1891) 571.

_____. "Personal Relations to the Question of Higher Criticism." *Christian Advocate* 79:11 (17 March 1904) 426-427.

Ury, M. William. *Trinitarian Personhood: Investigating the Implications of a Relational Definition*. Wipf & Stock, 2002.

Vanhoozer, Kevin J. *Remythologizing Theology: Divine Action, Passion, and Authorship*. Cambridge University Press, 2010.

Vargo, Kelly. "A Proleptic Feminist Wesley: Reflecting the Image of God in the Feminist and Wesleyan Places of Convergence." *Wesleyan Theological Journal* 55:1 (Spring 2020) 126-133.

Vermillion, William H. "1-2 Timothy, Titus." *Asbury Bible Commentary*. Eugene E. Carpenter and Wayne McCown, eds. Zondervan, 1992.

Wall, Robert W. *Revelation* in *New International Biblical Commentary*. W. Ward Gasque, ed. Peabody, MA: Henderson, 1991. [*NIBC*]

Weinrich, William. "Women in the History of the Church: Learned and Holy, But Not Pastors." *Recovering Biblical Manhood and Womanhood*. John Piper and Wayne Grudem, eds. Crossway, 1991. pp. 263-279.

Wenham, Gordon J. *Genesis 1-15: Word Biblical Commentary*. Word, 1987.

Wesley, John. *The Bicentennial Edition of the Works of John Wesley*. Frank Baker, ed. 35 vols. when complete. Abingdon, 1976–.

_____. *Explanatory Notes on the New Testament*. 1754. Reprint, Schmul, 1976.

Witherington, Ben III. "Why Arguments Against Women in Ministry Aren't Biblical. https://www.beliefnet.com/columnists/bibleandculture/2009/10/why-arguments-against-women-in-ministry-arent-biblical.html

Wynkoop, Mildred. *A Theology of Love*. Beacon Hill, 1972.

www.ingramcontent.com/pod-product-compliance
Lightning Source LLC
Chambersburg PA
CBHW060352050426
42449CB00011B/2953